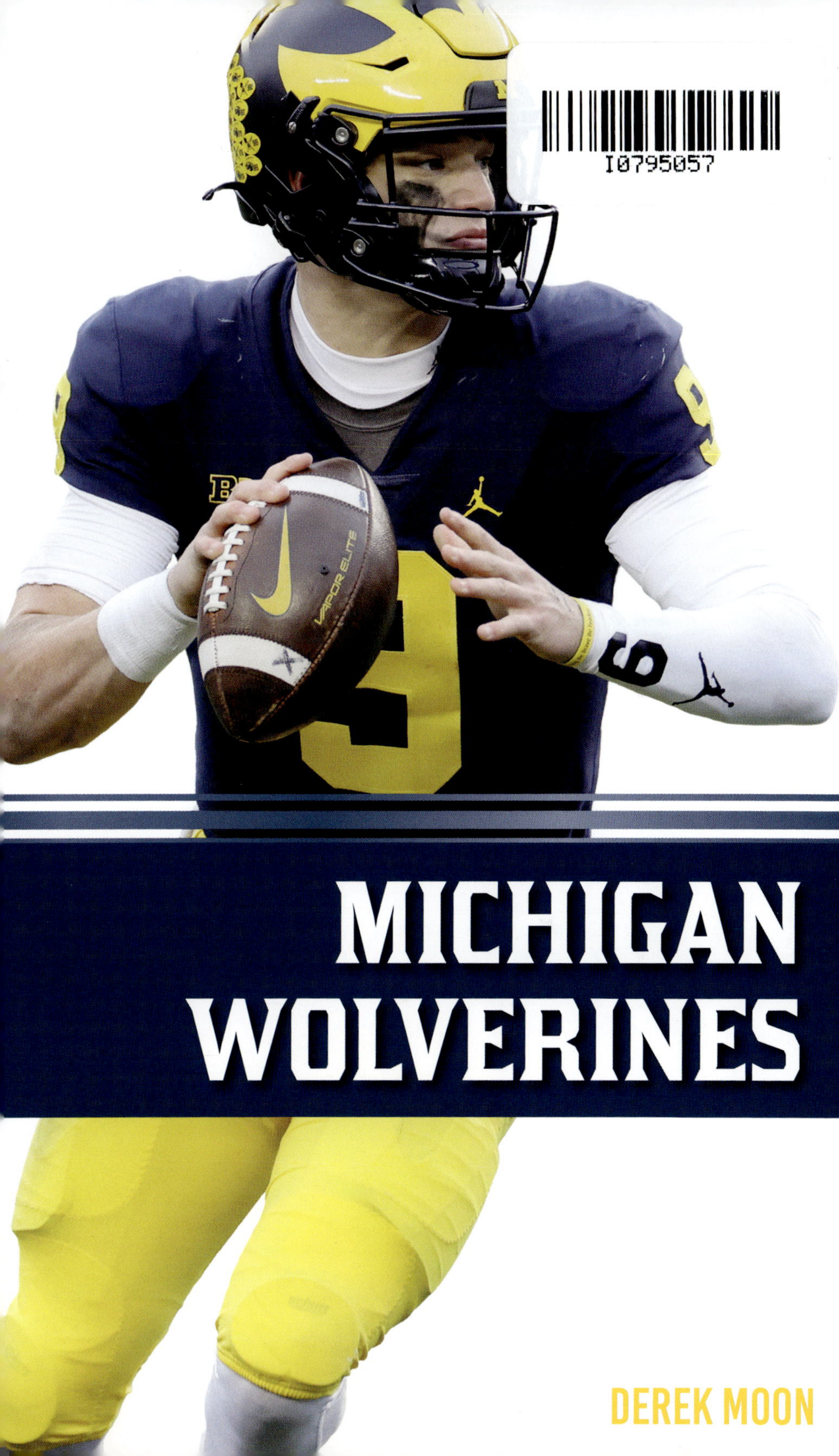

MICHIGAN WOLVERINES

DEREK MOON

WWW.APEXEDITIONS.COM

Apex is distributed by North Star Editions:
sales@northstareditions.com | 888-417-0195

Produced for Apex by Red Line Editorial.

Photographs ©: Joe Robbins/Icon Sportswire/AP Images, cover, 1; Aaron J. Thornton/Getty Images Sport/Getty Images, 4–5, 6–7, 50–51, 52–53; Bentley Historical Library/University of Michigan, 8–9; AP Images, 10–11, 12–13, 14–15, 16–17, 19, 20–21, 24–25; Harold Filan/AP Images, 22–23; Focus On Sport/Getty Images Sport/Getty Images, 26–27; Tom DiPace/AP Images, 28–29, 37, 57; George Widman/AP Images, 30–31; Gregory Shamus/Getty Images Sport/Getty Images, 32–33; CFP/Getty Images Sport/Getty Images, 34–35; Jonathan Daniel/Allsport/Getty Images Sport/Getty Images, 38–39; Tom Pidgeon/Getty Images Sport/Getty Images, 40–41; Dylan Buell/Getty Images Sport/Getty Images, 42–43; Shutterstock Images, 44–45, 58–59; Duane Burleson/AP Images, 47; G. Fiume/Getty Images Sport/Getty Images, 48–49; Ezra Shaw/Getty Images Sport/Getty Images, 54–55

Library of Congress Control Number: 2025930335

ISBN
979-8-89250-712-7 (hardcover)
979-8-89250-764-6 (paperback)
979-8-89250-747-9 (ebook pdf)
979-8-89250-730-1 (hosted ebook)

Printed in the United States of America
Mankato, MN
082025

NOTE TO PARENTS AND EDUCATORS

Apex books are designed to build literacy skills in striving readers. Exciting, high-interest content attracts and holds readers' attention. The text is carefully leveled to allow students to achieve success quickly.

TABLE OF CONTENTS

CHAPTER 1

GO BLUE!

A rumble goes through Michigan Stadium. The fans are on their feet. Soon, the band begins to play. Then the Michigan Wolverines charge onto the field. Their path takes them to a giant blue banner.

Michigan Stadium holds more than 107,000 fans.

Former Michigan athletes hold the banner high. It reads “Go Blue.” The players run under it. Game days in Ann Arbor, Michigan, are filled with traditions. And since 1962, every Wolverines home game has started just like this.

Each year, more than 100 student athletes play for Michigan's football team.

"THE VICTORS"

The Michigan Marching Band plays "The Victors" as the team takes the field. It's the school's fight song. The song dates back to 1898. A Michigan music student wrote it to celebrate a win.

CHAPTER 2

EARLY HISTORY

The University of Michigan was formed in 1837. The school's first football game took place in 1879. Michigan's rivalry with Ohio State began 18 years later. It's now one of the most famous rivalries in college football. Fans call their meetings "The Game."

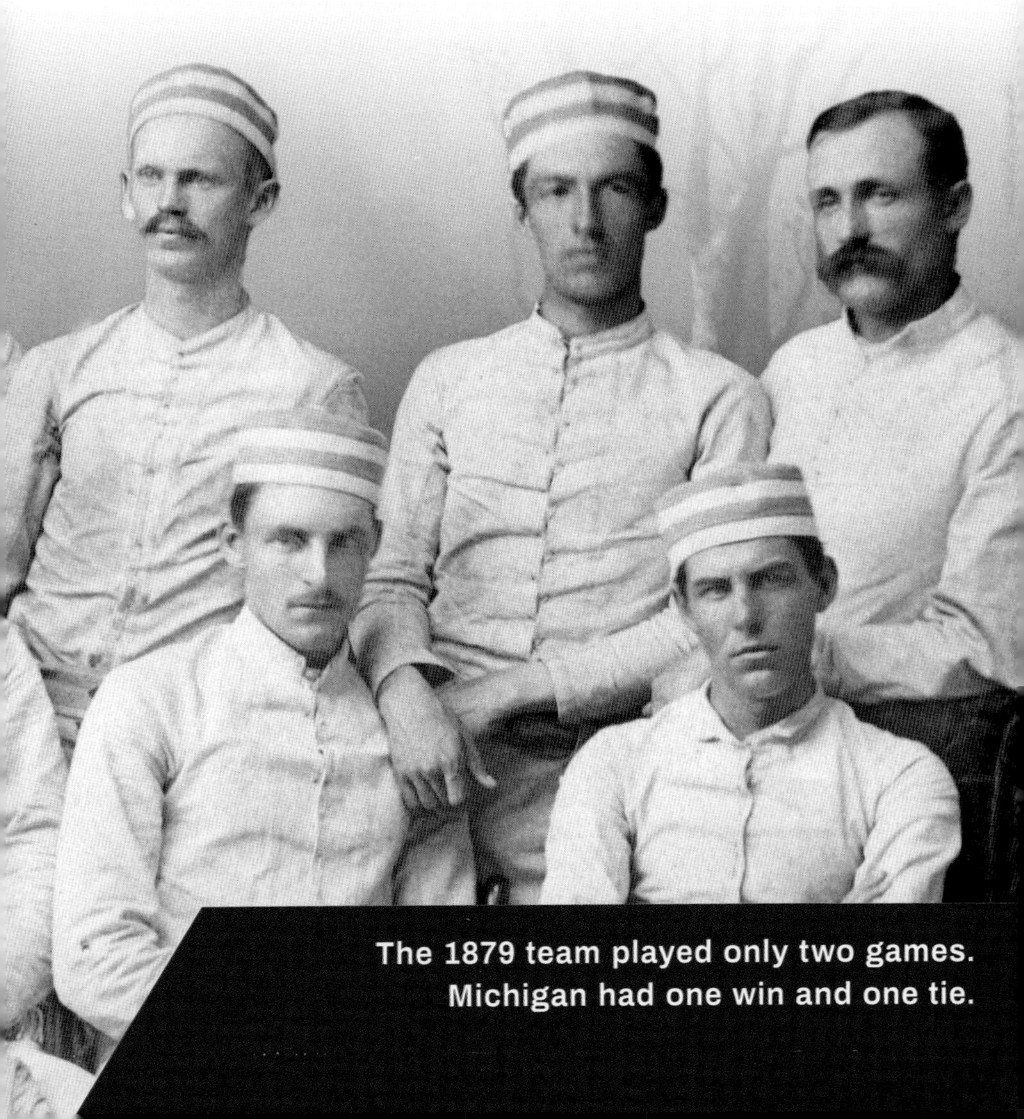

The 1879 team played only two games. Michigan had one win and one tie.

Early football looked more like rugby. But Michigan was very good. Fielding Yost became head coach in 1901. His teams played fast and scored often. Yost's first loss didn't come until 1905. He stepped down in 1926. By then, he had led Michigan to six national titles.

WOLVERINES

No one is sure why Michigan's team is called the Wolverines. The wolverine is a ferocious animal. But very few of them live in Michigan. Even so, students have been calling themselves Wolverines since the 1860s.

Fielding Yost's early teams scored so much they were nicknamed "Point-a-Minute."

Bob Chappuis led Michigan's offense in the 1947 season.

During the 1920s, college football grew into a major sport. The Wolverines remained one of the best teams. Michigan added two more national titles in the 1930s. The high-scoring 1947 team became known as the "Mad Magicians." The Wolverines shared the national title that year. Michigan's undefeated 1948 team won outright.

SNOW BOWL

A blizzard hit Ohio Stadium on November 25, 1950. Michigan and Ohio State played anyway. The Wolverines won the "Snow Bowl." The win earned Michigan a spot in the Rose Bowl.

Michigan fans tear down the goal posts to celebrate a 1969 win over Ohio State.

In the team's first 78 years, the Wolverines had just nine losing seasons. But from 1958 to 1967, they had six. A new coach arrived in 1969. Bo Schembechler's team was 7–2 when No. 1 Ohio State came to town. The Buckeyes had won 22 straight games. In a major upset, Michigan beat them 24–12.

ANOTHER SHOCKER

Michigan players helped Notre Dame start its football team in 1887. The schools played each other several times over the next few years. But their 1978 meeting was the first in 35 years. Notre Dame was the defending national champion. The Wolverines upset the Fighting Irish 28–14.

Players carry Schembechler off the field after a 1976 win over Ohio State.

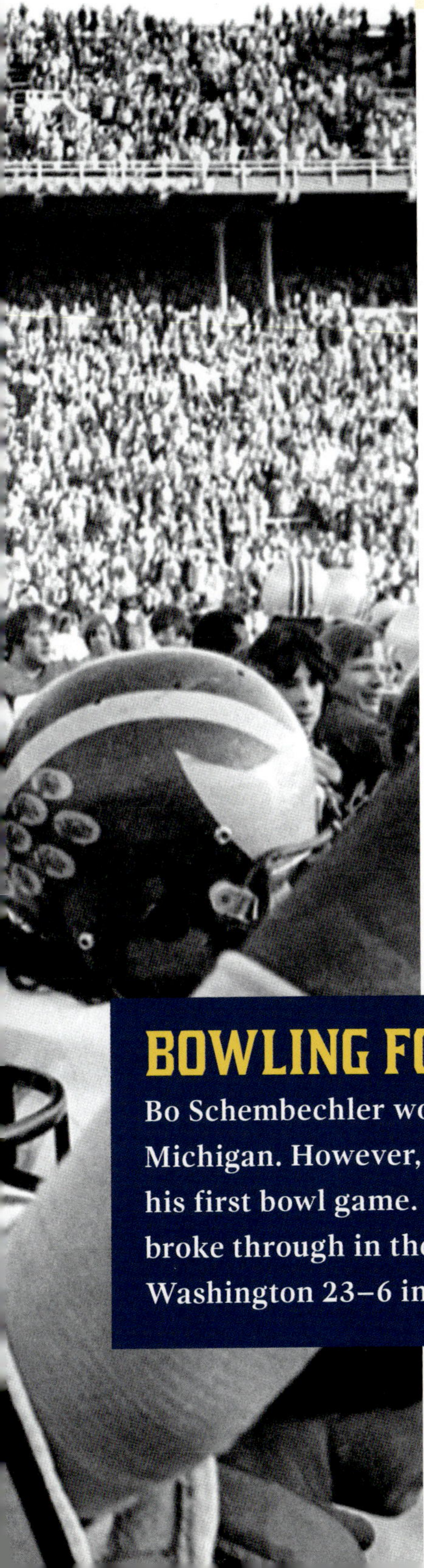

Schembechler turned Michigan into a force. Ohio State was already a power under coach Woody Hayes. The two coaches overlapped until 1978. Fans nicknamed this period the "Ten-Year War." The Wolverines came out ahead. They went 5–4–1 against the Buckeyes.

BOWLING FOR BO

Bo Schembechler won many games at Michigan. However, it took eight tries to win his first bowl game. His Wolverines finally broke through in the 1980 season. They beat Washington 23–6 in the Rose Bowl.

PLAYER SPOTLIGHT

TOM HARMON

Tom Harmon was known for big plays. The tailback could break free for long runs. He could also throw passes. Harmon even kicked field goals. It was no surprise that he led the nation in scoring in 1939. He did it again in 1940.

Harmon's last game against Ohio State was a blowout. He ran for three touchdowns. He threw for two more. Soon after, Harmon became Michigan's first Heisman Trophy winner. That award is given to the nation's best college football player.

IN HIS THREE YEARS AT MICHIGAN, TOM HARMON RAN FOR 30 TOUCHDOWNS AND THREW FOR 16 MORE.

CHAPTER 3

LEGENDS

Adolph Schulz played for the Wolverines in the early 1900s. He helped change the game of football. Schulz was the first center to snap the ball in a spiral. He also invented the linebacker position.

Adolph "Germany" Schulz served as Michigan's team captain in 1908.

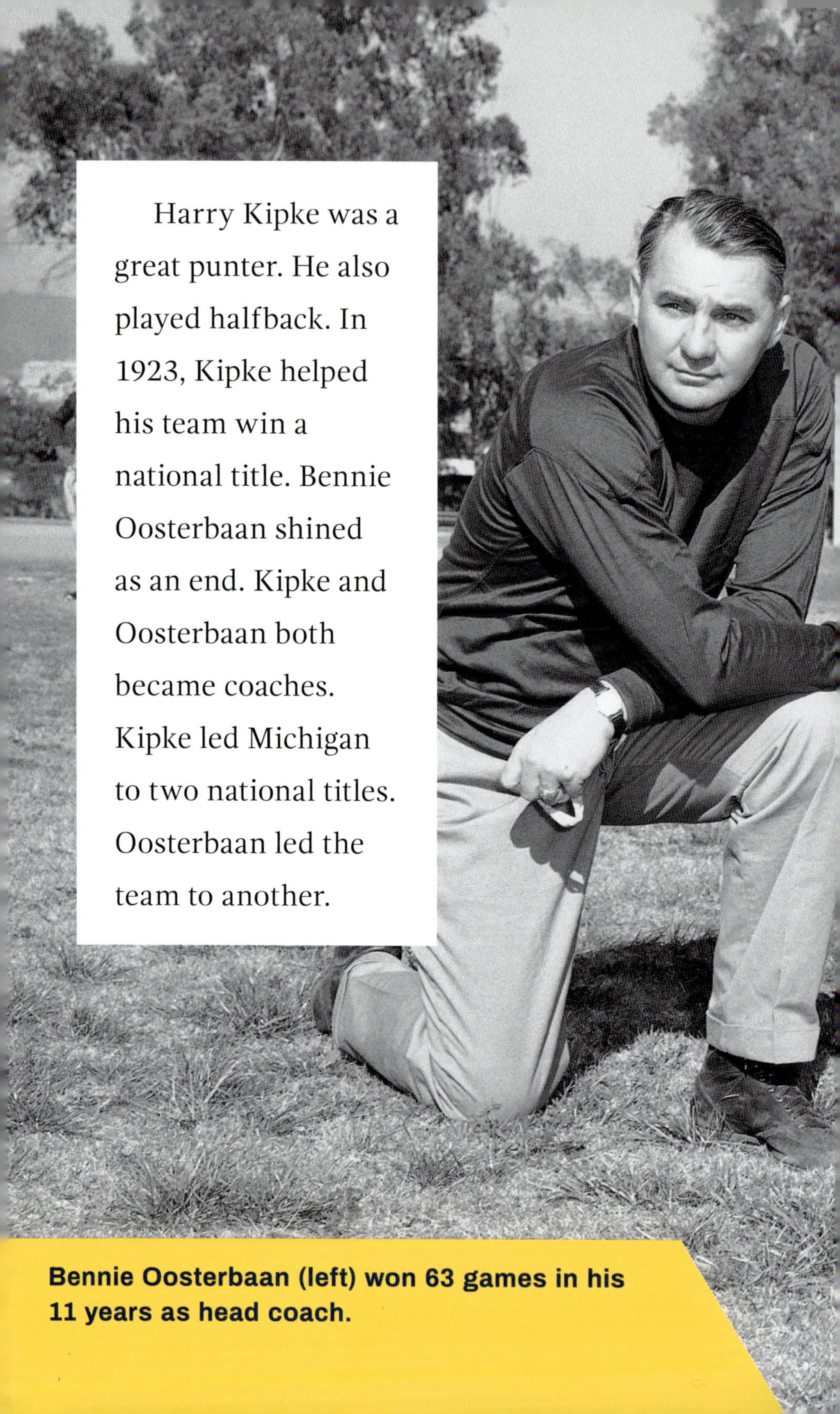

Harry Kipke was a great punter. He also played halfback. In 1923, Kipke helped his team win a national title. Bennie Oosterbaan shined as an end. Kipke and Oosterbaan both became coaches. Kipke led Michigan to two national titles. Oosterbaan led the team to another.

Bennie Oosterbaan (left) won 63 games in his 11 years as head coach.

THE WISTERT BROTHERS

Francis, Albert, and Alvin Wistert all played for Michigan in the 1930s and 1940s. All three brothers played tackle. And they all wore No. 11. Michigan later retired that number to honor the brothers.

Bob Chappuis tries to avoid a USC defender during the Rose Bowl on January 1, 1948.

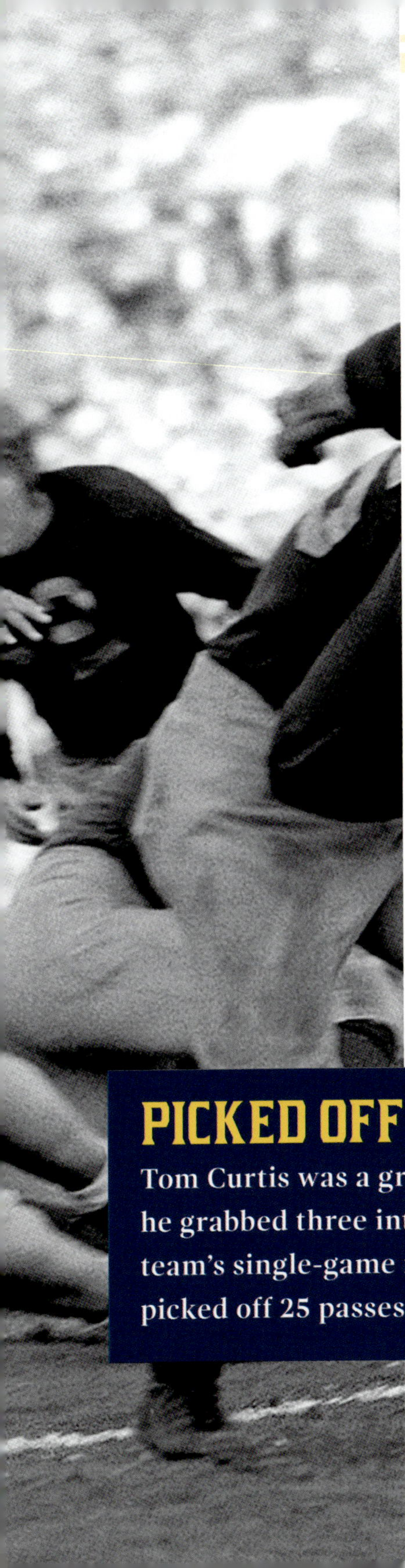

Bob Chappuis left college to fight in World War II (1939–1945). The halfback returned to Michigan in 1946. A year later, he helped the Wolverines go undefeated.

In the 1950s, Ron Kramer led Michigan with his hard-nosed play. Kramer starred on offense and defense.

PICKED OFF

Tom Curtis was a great safety. In a 1967 game, he grabbed three interceptions. That set the team's single-game record. In total, Curtis picked off 25 passes. That's also a team record.

Jim Harbaugh looks for a receiver during a 1986 game against Notre Dame.

Anthony Carter was short but fast. He caught just about any pass that came near him. Carter left Michigan after the 1982 season. At the time, he held most of the school's receiving records.

Fans remember Jim Harbaugh as one of Michigan's greatest quarterbacks. In 1986, he guaranteed Michigan would beat Ohio State. Then he backed it up. The Wolverines won 26–24. Harbaugh later coached the team. He led Michigan to the 2023 national title.

CHAPTER 4

RECENT HISTORY

The No. 3 Wolverines hosted No. 7 Notre Dame in September 1991. It was a close game. The Wolverines faced fourth-and-one late in the game. Desmond Howard made a diving touchdown grab. It sealed the win. The play became known as "The Catch."

In 1991, Desmond Howard led the nation with 19 touchdown catches.

Michigan defenders celebrate a sack during a 1997 game against Penn State.

Lloyd Carr took over as Michigan's coach in 1995. Two years later, the Wolverines had a dominant defense. Michigan arrived at the Rose Bowl undefeated. The Wolverines beat Washington State 21–16. Sportswriters named Michigan the national champion. However, the Coaches Poll picked Nebraska. Back then, there was no playoff. So, Michigan shared the national title.

Wide receiver Mario Manningham runs with the ball during a 2006 game against Ohio State.

Michigan remained a strong team. But it also faced some tough times. In 2007, the No. 5 Wolverines lost to Appalachian State. It was a shocking upset. Carr stepped down after that season. The team struggled to replace him. Meanwhile, Ohio State beat Michigan for the seventh time in a row in 2011.

GAME OF THE CENTURY

Michigan and Ohio State met in 2006. They were the nation's top two teams. The game was a thriller. Both teams put up huge numbers. However, the Buckeyes held on to win 42–39.

Jim Harbaugh took over as coach in 2015. In 2023, it all came together. Michigan met Washington for the national title. The Wolverines took an early lead. And they never gave it up. For the 12th time, the Wolverines were national champions.

TURNING THE TABLES

Between 2001 and 2019, Ohio State won 17 of 19 games against Michigan. The Wolverines got back on track in 2021. Michigan won again in 2022 and 2023. And in 2024, the Wolverines made it four straight wins.

Jim Harbaugh lifts the trophy after winning Michigan's 12th national title.

PLAYER SPOTLIGHT

DESMOND HOWARD

Michigan recruited Desmond Howard to play running back. Coaches then switched him to wide receiver. By his junior year in 1991, Howard was one of the sport's most electrifying players.

Howard scored 23 touchdowns that season. Most came on passes. But some came on runs and returns. Against Ohio State, Howard returned a punt 93 yards for a touchdown. To celebrate, he posed like the player on the Heisman Trophy. He won the award a few weeks later.

IN HIS 33 GAMES WITH MICHIGAN, HOWARD SCORED 35 TOUCHDOWNS.

MICHIGAN
21

CHAPTER 5

MODERN STARS

Michigan's 1997 team was loaded with talent. Offensive guard Steve Hutchinson didn't give up any sacks that season. That gave quarterback Brian Griese plenty of time. He whipped passes all around the field. Meanwhile, cornerback Charles Woodson led the team's defense.

Brian Griese threw for more than 2,000 yards in 1997.

In 2003, Chris Perry was named the country's top running back. A year later, receiver Braylon Edwards thrilled fans. In one game, Michigan trailed Michigan State by 17 points. Then Edwards scored two fourth-quarter touchdowns. And in triple overtime, he caught the winning touchdown.

COMEBACK WIN

Michigan faced Alabama in the Orange Bowl on January 1, 2000. It was the last game for Wolverines quarterback Tom Brady. Alabama led by 14 points. But Brady didn't give up. He led his team to an amazing 35–34 win.

Braylon Edwards scores a touchdown against Michigan State in 2004.

No offensive lineman has ever won the Heisman Trophy. Some fans thought Jake Long should have in 2007. Long blocked for quarterback Chad Henne. Henne set several Michigan passing records.

Aidan Hutchinson terrorized quarterbacks in 2021. The defensive end finished second in Heisman voting.

Aidan Hutchinson led the Big Ten with 14 sacks in 2021.

J. J. McCarthy started 28 games for Michigan. The Wolverines won 27 of them. McCarthy's passing helped lift Michigan to the 2023 national title.

Running back Blake Corum helped, too. He scored 27 rushing touchdowns in 2023. That set a school record.

BEST FOR LAST

Cornerback Will Johnson shut down receivers throughout 2023. He saved his best for the national title game. Johnson made a key interception. It helped Michigan pull away for the win.

Blake Corum (2) runs for a touchdown in the Rose Bowl on January 1, 2024.

PLAYER SPOTLIGHT

CHARLES WOODSON

In 1997, it seemed as if Charles Woodson did nothing but make big plays. He caught a 37-yard touchdown pass against Penn State. He returned a punt 78 yards for a score against Ohio State. However, most of his best plays came on defense. Woodson smothered opposing receivers. He picked off eight passes. On one, he caught the ball with one hand.

Woodson's play helped Michigan win a national title. He also became the first primarily defensive player to win the Heisman Trophy.

CHARLES WOODSON RECORDED 18 INTERCEPTIONS IN HIS THREE YEARS WITH MICHIGAN.

CHAPTER 6

TEAM TRIVIA

Michigan won its first football game in 1879. After that, the wins kept piling up. In November 2023, the Wolverines beat Maryland. That victory made Michigan the first college football team with 1,000 wins.

J. J. McCarthy fires a pass during Michigan's 1,000th win in school history.

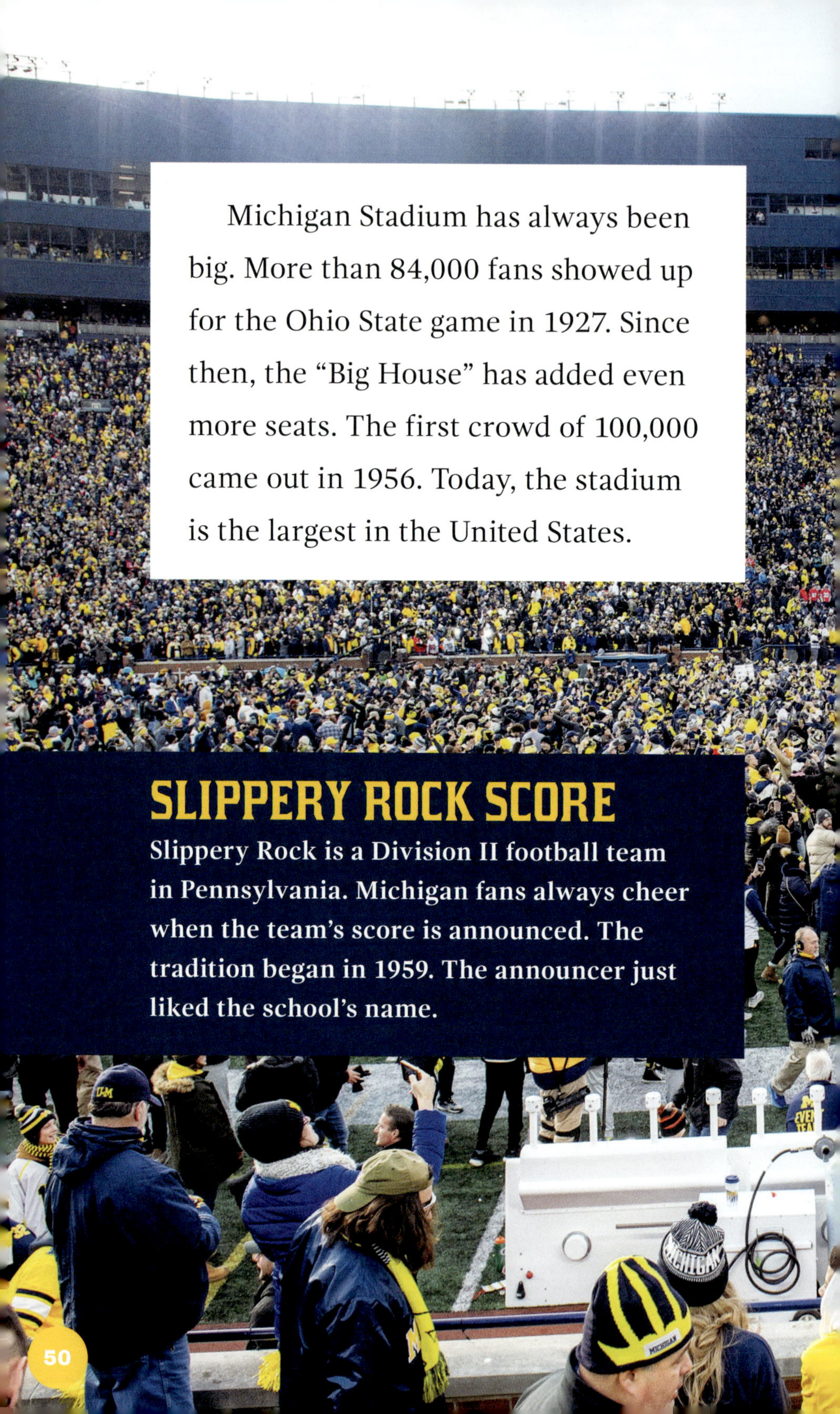

Michigan Stadium has always been big. More than 84,000 fans showed up for the Ohio State game in 1927. Since then, the "Big House" has added even more seats. The first crowd of 100,000 came out in 1956. Today, the stadium is the largest in the United States.

SLIPPERY ROCK SCORE

Slippery Rock is a Division II football team in Pennsylvania. Michigan fans always cheer when the team's score is announced. The tradition began in 1959. The announcer just liked the school's name.

Thousands of Michigan fans celebrate on the field after a 2023 win over Ohio State.

The Wolverines are impossible to miss. Their blue helmets feature three maize wings. It's an iconic look. Even some of Michigan's other sports teams use it. Coach Fritz Crisler introduced the design in 1938. He thought it would make receivers easier to see downfield.

NO. 1

At Michigan, the No. 1 jersey is special. It's saved for a game-changing wide receiver. However, a player must earn it. Some years, no one wears the number.

Roman Wilson sports the No. 1 jersey during the Rose Bowl on January 1, 2024.

Michigan fans wait all year for the Ohio State game. But the school has other great rivalries, too. The Wolverines first played Michigan State in 1898. Today, the winner gets the Paul Bunyan Trophy. The Wolverines also have a long history with Notre Dame. However, the schools no longer play every year.

LITTLE BROWN JUG

Michigan left its water jug in Minnesota after a 1903 game. The Gophers offered to give it back in 1909. But Michigan had to beat them first. Ever since, the winner gets to keep the Little Brown Jug.

Michigan usually plays Ohio State in the last game of the regular season.

TEAM RECORDS

All-Time Passing Yards: 9,715
Chad Henne (2004–07)

All-Time Rushing Yards: 5,040
Mike Hart (2004–07)

All-Time Receiving Yards: 3,541
Braylon Edwards (2001–04)

All-Time Touchdowns: 72
Willie Heston (1901–04)

All-Time Scoring: 356
Blake Corum (2020–23)

All-Time Interceptions: 25
Tom Curtis (1967–69)

All-Time Sacks: 36
Mark Messner (1985–88)

All-Time Tackles: 516
Ron Simpkins (1976–79)

All-Time Coaching Wins: 194
Bo Schembechler (1969–89)

Heisman Trophy Winners: 3
Tom Harmon (1940), Desmond Howard (1991), Charles Woodson (1997)

National Championships: 12
1901, 1902, 1903, 1904, 1918, 1923, 1932†, 1933, 1947†, 1948, 1997†, 2023

† *Season in which more than one school claims the national title.*

All statistics are accurate through 2024.

21

TIMELINE

1879
On May 30, Michigan plays its first game and beats Racine College.

1902
On January 1, Michigan beats Stanford 49–0 in the first Rose Bowl. The win lifts Michigan to the first of four straight national titles.

1926
Fielding Yost steps down after leading Michigan to six national championships.

1927
On October 1, Michigan thumps Ohio Wesleyan 33–0 in the first game at Michigan Stadium.

1940
Tailback Tom Harmon becomes Michigan's first Heisman Trophy winner.

1948

Michigan completes its second straight undefeated season and earns a second straight national title.

1978

On September 23, Michigan upsets defending national champion Notre Dame in the first meeting between the schools in 35 years.

1991

On November 23, Desmond Howard does the Heisman Trophy pose after scoring on a 93-yard punt return.

1998

On January 1, Michigan defeats Washington State in the Rose Bowl to clinch the school's first national title in 49 years.

2024

On January 8, Michigan beats Washington to claim the school's 12th national title.

COMPREHENSION QUESTIONS

Write your answers on a separate piece of paper.

1. Write a paragraph that explains the main ideas of Chapter 2.

2. Who do you think was the greatest player in Wolverines history? Why?

3. Who was Michigan's first Heisman Trophy winner?

   A. Adolph Schulz
   B. Tom Harmon
   C. Charles Woodson

4. Why is Michigan Stadium nicknamed the "Big House"?

   A. Many students live in the building.
   B. It is the country's largest stadium.
   C. It was used as a jail in the 1800s.

5. What does **recruited** mean in this book?

*Michigan **recruited** Desmond Howard to play running back. Coaches then switched him to wide receiver.*

A. caught a pass

B. scored a touchdown

C. asked someone to join a team

6. What does **smothered** mean in this book?

*Woodson **smothered** opposing receivers. He picked off eight passes.*

A. threw the ball toward

B. ran away from

C. covered closely

Answer key on page 64.

GLOSSARY

bowl game
A postseason college football game that successful teams are invited to take part in.

fight song
A song meant to inspire a school's sports teams.

iconic
Famous or well known.

interceptions
Passes that are caught by a defensive player.

overtime
An extra period that happens if two teams are tied at the end of the fourth quarter.

retired
Decided that a jersey number may no longer be worn by another player.

rivalry
An ongoing competition that brings out strong emotion from fans and players.

sacks
Plays that happen when a defender tackles the quarterback before he can throw the ball.

traditions
Ways of doing things that are passed down over many years.

upset
When a team wins a game that it was expected to lose.

TO LEARN MORE

BOOKS

Hanlon, Luke. *Tom Brady*. Abdo Publishing, 2024.

Kelley, K. C. *Michigan Wolverines*. The Child's World, 2022.

Ryan, Todd. *Michigan Wolverines*. Abdo Publishing, 2021.

ONLINE RESOURCES

Visit **www.apexeditions.com** to find links and resources related to this title.

ABOUT THE AUTHOR

Derek Moon is an author and avid Stratego player who lives in Watertown, Massachusetts, with his wife and daughter.

INDEX

ANSWER KEY:

1. Answers will vary; 2. Answers will vary; 3. B; 4. B; 5. C; 6.